Making Sacrifices
The Cost of Discipleship

STUDY GUIDE
by
Drew Gordon

FAITH
ALIVE®
Christian Resources

Grand Rapids, Michigan

Cover photo: The Image Bank

Unless otherwise indicated, the Scripture quotations in this publication are from the HOLY BIBLE, NEW INTERNATIONAL VERSION, © 1973, 1978, 1984, International Bible Society. Used by permission of Zondervan Bible Publishers.

Faith Alive Christian Resources published by CRC Publications. Discover Life series. *Making Sacrifices: The Cost of Discipleship*, © 2003 by CRC Publications, 2850 Kalamazoo Ave. SE, Grand Rapids, MI 49560. All rights reserved. With the exception of brief excerpts for review purposes, no part of this book may be reproduced in any manner whatsoever without written permission from the publisher. Printed in the United States of America on recycled paper.

We welcome your comments. Call us at 1-800-333-8300 or e-mail us at editors@faithaliveresources.org.

ISBN 1-56212-861-2

10 9 8 7 6 5 4 3 2 1

Contents

Introduction

Since I was always tall for my age, people assumed I'd be a natural at basketball. I loved the sport. But at age sixteen, I was a gawky giant who could scarcely jump and whose reactions were slow as molasses. I had little experience and a lot to learn—much of it learned from the bench.

When the new coach arrived my junior year of high school, everything changed. He taught the fundamentals to everyone—from grade schoolers to seniors. And he worked us hard—a lot of three and a half-hour practices for me, and basketball became a year-round sport. He was constantly testing us, stretching us, measuring our progress.

Without the quickness and natural ability of many other players, every practice was a challenge for me. It was a battle of me against myself, to see whether I would continue or give up. But if I was going to play the game, I wanted to be the best, and I wanted our team to win.

We did win. By the following year we were district champions and ranked in the top ten teams in the state. Three years later the coach took our high school to the state title with a perfect record of 30-0.

Though my basketball journey was grueling, I wouldn't have wanted it any other way. In fact, my college coaches were much less rigorous, and it made me angry! I wanted my team to be the best, if we were going to play at all.

I'm not sure, then, why the fact that the Christian life involves suffering came as such a shock. But this verse is in the Bible, and there is no escaping it: "Everyone who wants to live a godly life in Christ Jesus will be persecuted" (2 Tim. 3:12). The more that verse bothered my conscience, the more passages I found that repeated the same message. Suffering, trials, and persecution in the Christian life are normal!

Since that is the case, I wanted to find out more. I knew that God's way is always best, and so studying more about this subject would help me as I prepared for the long season ahead. I'm old enough to know that in order to reach a goal in life you must make sacrifices. I want my sacrifices to be for a goal that matters—now and for all time. Join me, won't you?

—*Drew Gordon*
Pittsburgh, Pennsylvania

Sacrifice in Moderation?

Lesson 1

Luke 5:9-11

⁹For [Simon Peter] and all his companions were astonished at the catch of fish they had taken, ¹⁰and so were James and John, the sons of Zebedee, Simon's partners.

Then Jesus said to Simon, ¹¹"Don't be afraid; from now on you will catch men." So they pulled their boats up on shore, left everything and followed him.

Matthew 19:16-30

¹⁶Now a man came up to Jesus and asked, "Teacher, what good thing must I do to get eternal life?"

¹⁷"Why do you ask me about what is good?" Jesus replied. "There is only One who is good. If you want to enter life, obey the commandments."

¹⁸"Which ones?" the man inquired.

Jesus replied, "'Do not murder, do not commit adultery, do not steal, do not give false testimony, ¹⁹honor your father and mother,' and 'love your neighbor as yourself.'"

²⁰"All these I have kept," the young man said. "What do I still lack?"

²¹Jesus answered, "If you want to be perfect, go, sell your possessions and give to the poor, and you will have treasure in heaven. Then come, follow me."

²²When the young man heard this, he went away sad, because he had great wealth.

²³Then Jesus said to his disciples, "I tell you the truth, it is hard for a rich man to enter the kingdom of heaven. ²⁴Again I tell you, it is easier for a camel to go through the eye of a needle than for a rich man to enter the kingdom of God."

²⁵When the disciples heard this, they were greatly astonished and asked, "Who then can be saved?"

²⁶Jesus looked at them and said, "With man this is impossible, but with God all things are possible."

²⁷Peter answered him, "We have left everything to follow you! What then will there be for us?"

²⁸Jesus said to them, "I tell you the truth, at the renewal of all things, when the Son of Man sits on his glorious throne, you who have followed me will also sit on twelve thrones, judging the twelve tribes of Israel. ²⁹And everyone who has left houses or brothers or sisters or father or mother or children or fields for my sake will receive a hundred times as much and will inherit eternal life. ³⁰But many who are first will be last, and many who are last will be first.

Luke 14:25-35

²⁵Large crowds were traveling with Jesus, and turning to them he said: ²⁶"If anyone comes to me and does not hate his father and mother, his wife and children, his brothers and sisters—yes, even his own life—he cannot be my disciple. ²⁷And anyone who does not carry his cross and follow me cannot be my disciple.

²⁸"Suppose one of you wants to build a tower. Will he not first sit down and estimate the cost to see if he has enough money to complete it? ²⁹For if he lays the foundation and is not able to finish it, everyone who sees it will ridicule him, ³⁰saying, 'This fellow began to build and was not able to finish.'

³¹"Or suppose a king is about to go to war against another king. Will he not first sit down and consider whether he is able with ten thousand men to oppose the one coming against him with twenty thousand? ³²If he is not able, he will send a delegation while the other is still a long way off and will ask for terms of peace. ³³In the same way, any of you who does not give up everything he has cannot be my disciple.

³⁴"Salt is good, but if it loses its saltiness, how can it be made salty again? ³⁵It is fit neither for the soil nor for the manure pile; it is thrown out.

"He who has ears to hear, let him hear."

STUDIES IN THIS SERIES

Questions

1. **Have you ever won a championship?**

2. **Luke 5:9-11**
   a. Why do you think the fishermen were afraid?
   b. How radical was Jesus' directive? How did his direction run parallel with their current occupation?
   c. What might be the consequences of leaving everything behind?

3. **Matthew 19:16-30**
   a. How would you describe the man who approached Jesus?
   b. What did Jesus say was the key to this man's quest?
   c. What was the man's response upon hearing the answer to his intensive search?
   d. What was the disciples' response to this incident?
   e. What did the disciples sacrifice? What did Jesus say other people had sacrificed?

4. **Luke 14:25-35**
   a. What examples show the length to which this commitment goes?
   b. Retell the "tower" illustration in terms of a big building project someone might undertake today.
   c. Retell the "kings" illustration in contemporary terms.
   d. How might verses 33-34 relate to the two illustrations?

5. **Summary**
   a. Almost everyone says they want to go to heaven. Based on your experience, what percentage of those would you guess have really counted the cost of getting there?
   b. What is the cost of following Jesus?
   c. When should a person consider the cost of following Jesus?

Planning for the Trip

Imagine your telephone rings one day and a pleasant voice says, "I'm a representative of Carol Joy Enterprises, and do you remember entering a drawing for a month-long, all-expenses-paid vacation to the English countryside? Guess what—you're the winner!

"Come to our offices tomorrow at 11 o'clock, and we'll give you the details," the representative says. That night you can hardly sleep. A free vacation!

The next morning you sit across the desk from the woman.

"Okay, on May 17, you have a 7:40 p.m. flight out of Kennedy airport, so you'll need to be there by 5:30," she says.

"Kennedy airport?" you ask with a frown. "I don't like Kennedy. It's really hard to get there from where I live, especially in rush hour. I thought I was getting a free vacation in England."

"Yes. It all starts by catching a flight from Kennedy," she replies. "You'll have to wait in several lines and have your luggage checked and show your passport, and then you'll be flying all night to London."

"I don't like the sound of this," you complain. "What if the plane goes down in the ocean?"

The woman rolls her eyes. "Look, it's not going to go down."

"Well, I get nervous in an airplane."

She ignores you. "And then when you get to Heathrow airport in London—"

"Wait a minute! You said I was going to the English countryside."

"Yes, well, first you have to stand in line at the customs checkpoint. When you finally get to the front, they'll ask you some questions and stamp your passport. Then you'll have to get your luggage and haul it to the bus, which will take you into the city to catch the train. It's a three-hour train ride to your hotel."

You're getting irritated. "I don't want to do all that," you insist. "I just want to go straight to the little English village."

At this point the woman is ready to disqualify you and pick another winner!

We have all met Christians who expect their trip to heaven to be one smooth ride from the time they accepted Christ straight to the pearly gates.... [However], trouble breaks loose in their lives, and all of a sudden they're crying, "Where is God? Nobody told me this was going to happen."

—JIM CYMBALA IN *LEADERSHIP*

What Self-Denial Isn't

Self-denial has its place in a Christian's life, but God doesn't ask you to choose what is most painful to you. If you followed this path you would soon ruin your health, reputation, business, and friendship.

Self-denial consists of bearing patiently all those things that God allows to pass into your life. If you don't refuse anything that comes in God's order, you are tasting of the cross of Jesus Christ.

—SIXTEENTH-CENTURY SPIRITUAL DIRECTOR FRANÇOIS FÉNELON

A World Without Trouble

What kind of world would it be if Christians never got sick? If they never fell? Never got burned? Never got into auto accidents? How long would it take for the insurance companies to figure out what was going on?

And how long would it take for other people to catch on? Before long we would have a religion of instant gratification, obvious to everyone. Christians would never go bankrupt. Their kids would never use drugs or run away from home. Their loved ones would never suffer. Do you know what would happen? You would destroy faith. You would destroy character. Religion would become a crass commercial venture (which it already is, for some). Is that what we want?

"No," we say. "I guess not. I guess what I want is not that God would act that way for everyone, all the time. I just want him to do it for *me*." How many times a day would God hear that pitiful, self-centered appeal? "Just for *me*, Lord. Just for *my* children. Just for *my* friends." Is that what we want? A world that runs on selfishness?

—D. JAMES KENNEDY IN *TURN IT TO GOLD* (SERVANT)

Don't Be Deceived

The only man who has the right to say that he is justified by grace alone is the man who has left all to follow Christ. Such a man knows that the call to discipleship is a gift of grace, and that the call is inseparable from the grace. But those who try to use this grace as a dispensation from following Christ are simply deceiving themselves.

—DIETRICH BONHOEFFER IN *THE COST OF DISCIPLESHIP* (MACMILLAN)

Giving Away: A Radical Idea

In *Holy Land: A Suburban Memoir*, author D. J. Waldie observes that the biggest drawback to living alone is having nobody to forgive. It is not that you don't get certain things—companionship, sex, somebody to share the chores—it is that you don't give to them. You are deprived of a great opportunity: to learn to love your neighbor as yourself.

This was a radical notion in Christ's time; it is radical now. It will always be radical because it is the hardest way, the most illogical way, the "unfairest" way—and the only way that can grant us the peace that passes all understanding.

In a way I can see only dimly, marriage is causing me to be freer with my time, my money, my affections. It is changing my heart, one molecule at a time, from stone to flesh. Day by day, hour by hour, minute by minute, it is giving me the opportunity to die to myself.

—HEATHER KING IN *CONTEXT* (FEB. 15, 1999)

Losses and Gains

Lesson 2

Matthew 13:44-46

⁴⁴"The kingdom of heaven is like treasure hidden in a field. When a man found it, he hid it again, and then in his joy went and sold all he had and bought that field.

⁴⁵"Again, the kingdom of heaven is like a merchant looking for fine pearls. ⁴⁶When he found one of great value, he went away and sold everything he had and bought it."

Colossians 3:1-10

¹Since, then, you have been raised with Christ, set your hearts on things above, where Christ is seated at the right hand of God. ²Set your minds on things above, not on earthly things. ³For you died, and your life is now hidden with Christ in God. ⁴When Christ, who is your life, appears, then you also will appear with him in glory.

⁵Put to death, therefore, whatever belongs to your earthly nature: sexual immorality, impurity, lust, evil desires and greed, which is idolatry. ⁶Because of these, the wrath of God is coming. ⁷You used to walk in these ways, in the life you once lived. ⁸But now you must rid yourselves of all such things as these: anger, rage, malice, slander, and filthy language from your lips. ⁹Do not lie to each other, since you have taken off your old self with its practices ¹⁰and have put on the new self, which is being renewed in knowledge in the image of its Creator.

Philippians 3:7-21

⁷But whatever was to my profit I now consider loss for the sake of Christ. ⁸What is more, I consider everything a loss compared to the surpassing greatness of knowing Christ Jesus my Lord, for whose sake I have lost all things. I consider them rubbish, that I may gain Christ ⁹and be found in him, not having a righteousness of my own that comes from the law, but that which is through faith in Christ— the righteousness that comes from God and is by faith. ¹⁰I want to know Christ and the power of his resurrection and the fellowship of sharing in his sufferings, becoming like him in his death, ¹¹and so, somehow, to attain to the resurrection from the dead.

¹²Not that I have already obtained all this, or have already been made perfect, but I press on to take hold of that for which Christ Jesus took hold of me. ¹³Brothers, I do not consider myself yet to have taken hold of it. But one thing I do: Forgetting what is behind and straining toward what is ahead, ¹⁴I press on toward the goal to win the prize for which God has called me heavenward in Christ Jesus.

¹⁵All of us who are mature should take such a view of things. And if on some point you think differently, that too God will make clear to you. ¹⁶Only let us live up to what we have already attained.

¹⁷Join with others in following my example, brothers, and take note of those who live according to the pattern we gave you. ¹⁸For, as I have often told you before and now say again even with tears, many live as enemies of the cross of Christ. ¹⁹Their destiny is destruction, their god is their stomach, and their glory is in their shame. Their mind is on earthly things. ²⁰But our citizenship is in heaven. And we eagerly await a Savior from there, the Lord Jesus Christ, ²¹who, by the power that enables him to bring everything under his control, will transform our lowly bodies so that they will be like his glorious body.

Questions

1. **How did your life change the first time you fell in love?**

2. **Matthew 13:44-46**
   a. What about these two stories is similar?
   b. According to Jesus, how valuable is the kingdom of heaven?

3. **Colossians 3:1-10**
   a. What happened to Christ after he died?
   b. How might a person "put to death" the things on this list?
   c. How many times have you committed the sins listed in verses 5-9? Take a few moments to silently review your involvement in each kind of sin.

4. **Philippians 3:7-21**
   a. In verses 7-11, what shows you that the writer is excited not about a religion but a relationship?
   b. The writer, Paul, is a man with a vision. What is that vision?
   c. Does Paul consider himself unique in this vision?

5. **Summary**
   a. Love. Vision. Passion. These things tell you a lot about what is important to a person. What was important to Paul?
   b. If you are a follower of Christ, how much of your week do you think of yourself as a citizen of heaven? Why?

afterWord

The Cost of Following

[Costly grace] is costly because it calls us to follow, and it is grace because it calls us to follow Jesus Christ. It is costly because it costs a man his life, and it is grace because it gives a man the only true life.

Unexpected Rules for Life's Race

It was a strange bicycle race. According to the story I read, the object of this race in India was to go the *shortest* distance possible within a specified time. At the start of the race, everyone cued up at the line. When the gun sounded all the bicycles, as best they could, stayed put. Racers were disqualified if they tipped over or one of their feet touched the ground. And so they would inch forward just enough to keep the bike balanced. When the time was up and another gun sounded, the person who had gone the farthest was the loser and the person closest to the starting line was the winner.

Imagine getting into that race and not understanding how the race works. When the race starts, you pedal as hard and fast as you possibly can. You're out of breath. You're sweating. You're delighted because the other racers are back there at the starting line. You're going to break the record. You think, *This is fantastic.* Don't let up. Push harder and faster and longer and stronger.

At last you hear the gun that ends the race, and you are delighted because you are unquestionably the winner. Except you are unquestionably the loser because you misunderstood how the race is run.

Jesus gives us the rules to the eternal race of life. The finish line is painted on the other side of our deaths, right in front of the throne of God himself. There you will be repaid at the resurrection of the righteous. The winning strategy for this life and for all eternity is caring about others and not about ourselves. It is letting others go first and not pushing to the front. It is giving without the expectation of getting in return. It is to be humble, like Jesus.

—LEITH ANDERSON IN THE SERMON "THE HEIGHT OF HUMILITY"

Wallowing in the Mud

My own experience is something like this. I am progressing along the path of life in my ordinary contentedly fallen and godless condition, absorbed in a merry meeting with my friends for the morrow or a bit of work that tickles my vanity today, a holiday or a new book, when suddenly a stab of abdominal pain that threatens serious disease, or a headline in the newspapers that threatens us all with destruction, sends this whole pack of cards tumbling down. At first I am overwhelmed, and all my little happinesses look like broken toys. Then, slowly and reluctantly, bit by bit, I try to bring myself into the frame of mind that I should be in at all times. I remind myself that all these toys were never intended to possess my heart, that my true good is in another world and my only real treasure is Christ. . . . Let [God] but sheathe that sword for a moment and I behave like a puppy when the hated bath is over—I shake myself as dry as I can and race off to reacquire my comfortable dirtiness, if not in the nearest manure heap, at least in the nearest flower bed. And that is why tribulations cannot cease until God either sees us remade or sees that our remaking is now hopeless.

—C. S. LEWIS IN *THE PROBLEM OF PAIN* (MACMILLAN)

Unselfish Intimacy

After Philip Yancey and his wife reached their 25th wedding anniversary, he reflected on their experience:

Before marriage, each by instinct strives to be what the other wants. The young woman desires to look sexy and takes up interest in sports. The young man notices plants and flowers, and works at asking questions instead of just answering monosyllabically. After marriage, the process slows and somewhat reverses. Each insists on his or her rights. Each resists bending to the other's will.

After years, though, the process may subtly begin to reverse again. I sense a new willingness to bend back toward what the other wants—maturely, this time, not out of a desire to catch a mate but out of a desire to please a man who has shared a quarter-century of life. I grieve for those couples who give up before reaching this stage.

—PHILIP YANCEY IN *MARRIAGE PARTNERSHIP*

So You Want to Be Like Jesus (Part 1)

Psalm 22:1-18

¹My God, my God, why have you forsaken me?
   Why are you so far from saving me,
   so far from the words of my groaning?
²O my God, I cry out by day, but you do not answer,
   by night, and am not silent.
³Yet you are enthroned as the Holy One;
   you are the praise of Israel.
⁴In you our fathers put their trust;
   they trusted and you delivered them.
⁵They cried to you and were saved;
   in you they trusted and were not disappointed.
⁶But I am a worm and not a man,
   scorned by men and despised by the people.
⁷All who see me mock me;
   they hurl insults, shaking their heads:
⁸"He trusts in the LORD;
   let the LORD rescue him.
Let him deliver him,
   since he delights in him."
⁹Yet you brought me out of the womb;
   you made me trust in you
   even at my mother's breast.
¹⁰From birth I was cast upon you;
   from my mother's womb you have been my God.
¹¹Do not be far from me,
   for trouble is near
   and there is no one to help.
¹²Many bulls surround me;
   strong bulls of Bashan encircle me.
¹³Roaring lions tearing their prey
   open their mouths wide against me.
¹⁴I am poured out like water,
   and all my bones are out of joint.
My heart has turned to wax;
   it has melted away within me.
¹⁵My strength is dried up like a potsherd,
   and my tongue sticks to the roof of my mouth;
   you lay me in the dust of death.
¹⁶Dogs have surrounded me;
   a band of evil men has encircled me,
   they have pierced my hands and my feet.
¹⁷I can count all my bones;
   people stare and gloat over me.
¹⁸They divide my garments among them
   and cast lots for my clothing.

1 Peter 2:19-25

¹⁹For it is commendable if a man bears up under the pain of unjust suffering because he is conscious of God. ²⁰But how is it to your credit if you receive a beating for doing wrong and endure it? But if you suffer for doing good and you endure it, this is commendable before God. ²¹To this you were called, because Christ suffered for you, leaving you an example, that you should follow in his steps.

²²"He committed no sin,
   and no deceit was found in his mouth."

²³When they hurled their insults at him, he did not retaliate; when he suffered, he made no threats. Instead, he entrusted himself to him who judges justly. ²⁴He himself bore our sins in his body on the tree, so that we might die to sins and live for righteousness; by his wounds you have been healed. ²⁵For you were like sheep going astray, but now you have returned to the Shepherd and Overseer of your souls.

Hebrews 2:10

In bringing many sons to glory, it was fitting that God, for whom and through whom everything exists, should make the author of their salvation perfect through suffering.

Luke 9:22-26

²²And he said, "The Son of Man must suffer many things and be rejected by the elders, chief priests and teachers of the law, and he must be killed and on the third day be raised to life."

²³Then he said to them all: "If anyone would come after me, he must deny himself and take up his cross daily and follow me. ²⁴For whoever wants to save his life will lose it, but whoever loses his life for me will save it. ²⁵What good is it for a man to gain the whole world, and yet lose or forfeit his very self? ²⁶If anyone is ashamed of me and my words, the Son of Man will be ashamed of him when he comes in his glory and in the glory of the Father and of the holy angels."

Questions

1. **When you think about Jesus as he lived on earth, what comes to your mind?**

2. **Psalm 22:1-18**
   a. What feelings come over you as you hear this passage?
   b. Have you ever felt, as this writer did, that God had forsaken you?
   c. What things show how desperate this situation is?
   d. For those who know something about the story of Jesus' crucifixion, what parallels do you see in this passage?
   e. What does the writer know to be true about God?

3. **1 Peter 2:19-25**
   a. What kind of suffering and response to suffering are worthy of commendation?
   b. According to this passage, what is our calling?
   c. In what ways does this passage show that Christ suffered unjustly?

4. **Hebrews 2:10**
   a. Who is the "author of their salvation"?
   b. What right did God have to make him suffer?
   c. According to this verse, what purpose did God have in this suffering?

(continued on next page)

5. **Luke 9:22-26**
   a. How much did Jesus know about what lay ahead (vv. 22, 26)?
   b. Explain in your own words what a follower of Christ must do.

6. **Summary**
   a. How much does Jesus know about a life of suffering?
   b. What have you learned about suffering from today's study?

afterWord

Jesus Gave Everything

Mark's teacher called in the middle of the afternoon. His mother answered the phone.

"Mrs. Smith, your son did something in class that surprised me so much that I thought you should know about it immediately." The mother grew worried. Her third-grader was usually well-behaved.

"Nothing like this has happened in all my years of teaching," the woman continued. "This morning I was teaching a lesson on creative writing. And as I always do, I told the story of the ant and the grasshopper." She recounted the story as she had in class:

"The ant works hard all summer and stores up plenty of food. But the grasshopper plays all summer and does no work. Then winter comes. The grasshopper begins to starve because he has no food. So he begins to beg, 'Please Mr. Ant, you have much food. Please let me eat, too.' Then I said, 'Boys and girls, your job is to write the ending to the story.'

"Your son, Mark, raised his hand. 'Teacher, may I draw a picture?'

"I said, 'Well, yes, Mark, if you like, you may draw a picture. But first you must write the ending to the story.'

"As in all the years past, most of the students said that the ant shared his food through the winter and

both the ant and the grasshopper lived. A few children wrote, "No, Mr. Grasshopper. You should have worked in the summer. Now, I have just enough food for myself." So the ant lived and the grasshopper died.'

"But your son ended the story in a way different from any other child, ever. He wrote, 'So the ant gave all of his food to the grasshopper. The grasshopper lived through the winter, but the ant died.'

"And the picture? At the bottom of the page, Mark had drawn three crosses."

—*LEADERSHIP*

Where Was God?

A distraught father who was deeply grieved by the death of his son went to see his pastor and in bewildered anger said, "Where was God when my son died?" The pastor replied with a calm spirit, "The same place he was when his Son died."

—R. C. SPROUL IN *SURPRISED BY SUFFERING* (TYNDALE)

Imitating Christ

If pain sometimes shatters the creature's false self-sufficiency, yet in supreme "Trial" or "Sacrifice" it teaches him the self-sufficiency which really ought to be his—the "strength, which, if Heaven gave it, may be called his own," for then in the absence of all merely natural motives and supports, he acts in that strength, and that alone, which God confers upon him through his subjected will. Human will becomes truly creative and truly our own when it is wholly God's, and this is one of the many senses in which he that loses his soul shall find it. In all other acts our will is fed through nature, that is, through created things other than the self—through the desires which our physical organism and our heredity supply to us. When we act from ourselves alone—that is, from God *in* ourselves—we are collaborators in, or live instruments of, creation and that is why such an act undoes with "backward mutters of dissevering power" the uncreative spell which Adam laid upon his species.

Hence as suicide is the typical expression of the stoic spirit, and battle of the warrior spirit, martyrdom always remains the supreme enacting and perfection of Christianity. This great action has been initiated for us, done on our behalf, exemplified for our imitation, and inconceivably communicated to all believers, by Christ on Calvary.

—C. S. LEWIS IN *THE PROBLEM OF PAIN* (MACMILLAN)

Joy in Throwing Away

But where has my freedom been for so long?
From what secret depths was I dragged out
in an instant
that I might agree to bow my head
beneath your yoke which is gentle
and accept on my shoulder your burden
which is light,
O Lord Jesus Christ,
my strength and my redeemer?

How suddenly comforting it was to lose the false comforts of the past!
I had long feared losing them, and now it was a joy to throw them away.

Truly it was you who put them far from me,
my true and supreme comfort;
You put them far away
and set yourself in their place.

—SAINT AUGUSTINE, *THE CONFESSIONS 9.1*

Get Serious

If our Christianity has ceased to be serious about discipleship, if we have watered down the gospel into emotional uplift which makes no costly demands and which fails to distinguish between natural and Christian existence, then we cannot help regarding the cross as an ordinary everyday calamity, as one of the trials and tribulations of life.

—DIETRICH BONHOEFFER IN *THE COST OF DISCIPLESHIP* (MACMILLAN)

So You Want to Be Like Jesus (Part 2)

1 Peter 4:1-6

[1]Therefore, since Christ suffered in his body, arm yourselves also with the same attitude, because he who has suffered in his body is done with sin. [2]As a result, he does not live the rest of his earthly life for evil human desires, but rather for the will of God. [3]For you have spent enough time in the past doing what pagans choose to do—living in debauchery, lust, drunkenness, orgies, carousing and detestable idolatry. [4]They think it strange that you do not plunge with them into the same flood of dissipation, and they heap abuse on you. [5]But they will have to give account to him who is ready to judge the living and the dead. [6]For this is the reason the gospel was preached even to those who are now dead, so that they might be judged according to men in regard to the body, but live according to God in regard to the spirit. *live in the Spirit as God does*

[handwritten: punished with death] [handwritten: bodies]

1 Peter 4:12-17

[12]Dear friends, do not be surprised at the painful trial you are suffering, as though something strange were happening to you. [13]But rejoice that you participate in the sufferings of Christ, so that you may be overjoyed when his glory is revealed. [14]If you are insulted because of the name of Christ, you are blessed, for the Spirit of glory and of God rests on you. [15]If you suffer, it should not be as a murderer or thief or any other kind of criminal, or even as a meddler. [16]However, if you suffer as a Christian, do not be ashamed, but praise God that you bear that name. [17]For it is time for judgment to begin with the family of God; and if it begins with us, what will the outcome be for those who do not obey the gospel of God?

John 15:18-25

[18]"If the world hates you, keep in mind that it hated me first. [19]If you belonged to the world, it would love you as its own. As it is, you do not belong to the world, but I have chosen you out of the world. That is why the world hates you. [20]Remember the words I spoke to you: 'No servant is greater than his master.' If they persecuted me, they will persecute you also. If they obeyed my teaching, they will obey yours also. [21]They will treat you this way because of my name, for they do not know the One who sent me. [22]If I had not come and spoken to them, they would not be guilty of sin. Now, however, they have no excuse for their sin. [23]He who hates me hates my Father as well. [24]If I had not done among them what no one else did, they would not be guilty of sin. But now they have seen these miracles, and yet they have hated both me and my Father. [25]But this is to fulfill what is written in their Law: 'They hated me without reason.'"

2 Timothy 1:8-12

[8]So do not be ashamed to testify about our Lord, or ashamed of me his prisoner. But join with me in suffering for the gospel, by the power of God, [9]who has saved us and called us to a holy life—not because of anything we have done but because of his own purpose and grace. This grace was given us in Christ Jesus before the beginning of time, [10]but it has now been revealed through the appearing of our Savior, Christ Jesus, who has destroyed death and has brought life and immortality to light through the gospel. [11]And of this gospel I was appointed a herald and an apostle and a teacher. [12]That is why I am suffering as I am. Yet I am not ashamed, because I know whom I have believed, and am convinced that he is able to guard what I have entrusted to him for that day.

Questions

1. **Have you ever been criticized or ridiculed for doing the right thing?**

2. **1 Peter 4:1-6**
   a. How should our attitude be like Christ's? *DO THE WILL OF GOD AND TO SUFFER FOR IT IF NESSESARY*
   b. How should our choices be different than the pagans'?
   c. What is a reason we share the gospel with people?

3. **1 Peter 4:12-17**
   a. How do you respond to having the flu? To being hospitalized? To being hurt in an athletic contest? To being ridiculed by someone?
   b. What reasons are given for joy and satisfaction when suffering?
   c. What kinds of suffering do not bring joy and blessings?
   d. Why do you think the passages about suffering for Christ often mention the coming judgment day?

4. **John 15:18-25**
   a. What reasons are given for the persecution of Christians?
   b. Should we take persecution personally?
   c. How is a person worse off if they see your testimony and reject it?

5. **2 Timothy 1:8-12**
   a. Have you ever felt embarrassed about being a Christian?
   b. What calling do we have?
   c. Why is Paul confident?

6. **Summary**
   a. Explain why being a follower of Christ means more than being a good person.
   b. What effect will our following Christ have on other people?
   c. In what ways is suffering a good thing?

You Can't Earn Sacrifice

As a former Army Ranger, Seattle pastor Tom Allen described a special connection he felt to the characters in the World War II movie *Saving Private Ryan:*

I was extremely proud—until the last minute of the movie. I was proud watching the Rangers take Omaha Beach. Then they receive a mission to go deep into enemy territory to save Private Ryan. They hit skirmish after skirmish, and some of them are killed along the way. They finally get to where Private Ryan is holed up, and they say, "Come with us. We've come to save you."

He says, "I'm not going. I have to stay here because there's a big battle coming up, and if I leave my men they're all going to die."

What do the Rangers say? "We'll stay here and fight with you."

They stay and fight, and it's gory and hard, and almost everyone dies except Private Ryan. At the end, one of the main characters—played by Tom Hanks—is sitting on the ground. He's been shot and he's dying. The battle has been won.

Private Ryan leans over to him, and Hanks whispers something to him. Everyone in the theater is crying because Tom Hanks was shot; I was crying because of what he said—it was so terrible. Ryan bent down and Hanks said, "Earn this."

The reason that made me angry is no Ranger would ever say, "Earn this." Why? Because the Ranger motto for the last 200 years has not been "earn this." The Ranger motto for the past 200 years has been *Sua sponte,* "I chose this." I volunteered for this.

If Hanks were really a Ranger he would have said, *"Sua sponte.* In other words, "This is free. You don't pay anything for this. I give up my life for you. That's my job."

And so when you look at the cross and see Jesus hanging there and hear him say, "I thirst," you do not hear "earn this." You never hear Jesus say, "Earn this." He doesn't say, "I've given everything up, everything for you. Now you need to gut it out for me."

What he says is "I thirst." He says, *"Sua sponte.* I volunteered for this. You don't have to pay anything for it."

—*PREACHING TODAY*

> "We make a living by what we get. We make a life by what we give."
>
> —WINSTON CHURCHILL

Losing Life, Finding It

Those who would bear the name *Chrisian* credibly experience a tremendous amount of abandonment in life. . . . If Christians are truly willing to leave everything to follow [Jesus], then they will, in fact, eventually leave everything. Either voluntarily or involuntarily, either by design or by accident, a day will come when they realize they have only Jesus. If he alone is savior, then we can find our lives only in being his disciples.

We have to abandon all hope that we can hang on to any other dream, any other relationship, any other vocation. For most of us this is asking too much. Given the choice between selling everything to blindly follow Jesus or returning sadly to our old life, we will choose the latter every time. That is why grace often comes in severe ways. We really don't have to seek abandonment. It finds us easily enough. Usually it comes as God's uninvited angel with the announcement of "good news" that we are about to lose our lives. In one way or another most of us have met that angel. The question is, Can we lean into the abandonment? Can we accept it as the Savior's invitation to find our lives at long last?

We will probably spend most of life with family, friends, good health, and good work. But they are not ours by rights. They are not promised to us. We may have to give them back to God at any moment. Someday we will give them back. The trick is to learn how to do that before they leave us. That allows us to spend the rest of our time enjoying them as the temporary gifts that they are.

—M. CRAIG BARNES IN *WHEN GOD INTERRUPTS* (INTERVARSITY PRESS)

Rewards of the Cross

To go one's way under the sign of the cross is not misery and desperation, but peace and refreshment for the soul; it is the highest joy. Then we do not walk under our self-made laws and burdens, but under the yoke of him who knows us and who walks under the yoke with us. Under his yoke we are certain of his nearness and communion. It is he whom the disciple finds as he lifts up his cross.

—DIETRICH BONHOEFFER IN *THE COST OF DISCIPLESHIP* (MACMILLAN)

2 Timothy 2:3-10

³Endure hardship with us like a good soldier of Christ Jesus. ⁴No one serving as a soldier gets involved in civilian affairs—he wants to please his commanding officer. ⁵Similarly, if anyone competes as an athlete, he does not receive the victor's crown unless he competes according to the rules. ⁶The hardworking farmer should be the first to receive a share of the crops. ⁷Reflect on what I am saying, for the Lord will give you insight into all this.

⁸Remember Jesus Christ, raised from the dead, descended from David. This is my gospel, ⁹for which I am suffering even to the point of being chained like a criminal. But God's word is not chained. ¹⁰Therefore I endure everything for the sake of the elect, that they too may obtain the salvation that is in Christ Jesus, with eternal glory.

James 1:2-4, 12

²Consider it pure joy, my brothers, whenever you face trials of many kinds, ³because you know that the testing of your faith develops perseverance. ⁴Perseverance must finish its work so that you may be mature and complete, not lacking anything.

¹²Blessed is the man who perseveres under trial, because when he has stood the test, he will receive the crown of life that God has promised to those who love him.

Hebrews 10:32-39

³²Remember those earlier days after you had received the light, when you stood your ground in a great contest in the face of suffering. ³³Sometimes you were publicly exposed to insult and persecution; at other times you stood side by side with those who were so treated. ³⁴You sympathized with those in prison and joyfully accepted the confiscation of your property, because you knew that you yourselves had better and lasting possessions.

³⁵So do not throw away your confidence; it will be richly rewarded. ³⁶You need to persevere so that when you have done the will of God, you will receive what he has promised. ³⁷For in just a very little while,

"He who is coming will come
   and will not delay.
³⁸But my righteous one will
   live by faith.
And if he shrinks back,
   I will not be pleased with
   him."

³⁹But we are not of those who shrink back and are destroyed, but of those who believe and are saved.

2 Corinthians 1:3-11

³Praise be to the God and Father of our Lord Jesus Christ, the Father of compassion and the God of all comfort, ⁴who comforts us in all our troubles, so that we can comfort those in any trouble with the comfort we ourselves have received from God. ⁵For just as the sufferings of Christ flow over into our lives, so also through Christ our comfort overflows. ⁶If we are distressed, it is for your comfort and salvation; if we are comforted, it is for your comfort, which produces in you patient endurance of the same sufferings we suffer. ⁷And our hope for you is firm, because we know that just as you share in our sufferings, so also you share in our comfort.

⁸We do not want you to be uninformed, brothers, about the hardships we suffered in the province of Asia. We were under great pressure, far beyond our ability to endure, so that we despaired even of life. ⁹Indeed, in our hearts we felt the sentence of death. But this happened that we might not rely on ourselves but on God, who raises the dead. ¹⁰He has delivered us from such a deadly peril, and he will deliver us. On him we have set our hope that he will continue to deliver us, ¹¹as you help us by your prayers. Then many will give thanks on our behalf for the gracious favor granted us in answer to the prayers of many.

Questions

1. **Can you remember a decision in your life that other people thought was crazy, but that you knew would have a good outcome?**

2. **2 Timothy 2:3-10**
   a. What displeases a commanding officer?
   b. What qualifies an athlete for victory?
   c. What sort of farmer deserves the first fruits of his crops?
   d. For what is Paul suffering?
   e. Why is Paul willing to endure anything?

3. **James 1:2-4, 12**
   a. In what ways do trials result in personal benefits here on earth?
   b. What eternal reward awaits the one who endures the trials?

4. **Hebrews 10:32-39**
   a. What trials had these people gone through?
   b. Why do these people seem to be at a turning point?
   c. What do they have to look forward to?

5. **2 Corinthians 1:3-11**
   a. Where does comfort come from?
   b. How does our suffering help others?
   c. How serious were the trials that the authors of this passage had suffered?
   d. How had the authors' past experiences with suffering affected their faith?

6. **Summary**
   a. How many benefits can you think of that can result from a Christian's suffering?
   b. Why does suffering through trials seem to enhance some people's character and to destroy other people's?

He Kept Coming Back

Charles Spurgeon once said, "By perseverance, the snail reached the ark!" I don't know whether an unknown missionary laboring in the Philippines a generation ago ever heard that, but I know he believed it. Laboring in a Catholic country where, a generation ago, Protestant missionaries were not always appreciated, he began to tell Anacleto Lacanilao that he needed to be born again and have a personal relationship with Jesus Christ. Lacanilao, who was the father of eight children, didn't buy this new concept and shrugged off the witness of his friend, who wasn't rebuffed but just kept coming back. Seven, eight, nine times the missionary came to the Lacanilao home and urged him to invite Jesus Christ into his life.

On the eleventh visit, Lacanilao told the unwelcome visitor, "If you come back one more time, I'm going to kill you!" It was not idle talk when he made that threat. And what happened? The man came back the twelfth time! Suppose someone told you, "If you talk to me one more time about Jesus Christ, I am going to kill you," what would you do? A lot of folks would assume that it might not be too healthy, but not the man who witnessed to Anacleto Lacanilao, because he came back the twelfth time and that was when Dad Lacanilao became a believer in Jesus Christ. He later said, "When he came back the twelfth time, I figured there must be something to this experience he was talking about, and I had better listen to him!"

Today, he and his wife are both in heaven, but their eight children are all serving the Lord, some as outstanding Christian leaders in the Philippines and the United States. One of the sons is Mike Lacanilao, former president of FEBIAS College of the Bible and head of Back to the Bible Ministries in the Philippines. Another served as head of Youth for Christ; but all of the eight children followed in the footsteps of Mom and Dad Lacanilao. It all happened because a faithful witness, whose name is unknown to me, didn't stop when he faced opposition.

—HAROLD J. SALA IN *HEROES: PEOPLE WHO MADE A DIFFERENCE IN OUR WORLD* (PROMISE PRESS)

More Money, More Gratitude?

Poorer Americans give a greater percentage of their income to charity. A recent study reveals that those who

- earned under $10,000 gave 5.2%,
- earned $10,000 to $19,999 gave 3.3%
- earned $75,000 to $99,999 gave only 1.6%.

—*TIME* (JULY 24, 2000)

Set Free

The disciples once asked Jesus whose sin was responsible for a man being born blind. It's the kind of question we ponder as well. Who is responsible for my problem? Whom should I blame? Or sue? But those questions will never help us find salvation. Even if we find someone to blame, we still haven't done anything about the problem. In fact, we've probably made it worse.

Unless it leads to forgiveness, assigning blame only turns the blamer into a victim.

The real question, Jesus said, is not "Who is responsible for the man's blindness?" but "Who can heal him?" Then, restoring the man's vision, Jesus said, "He was born blind so that God's works may be revealed in him." If we pray for vision, we can always see God at work in the broken places of life even if the wound, disease, or heartache remains. Seeing that God is with us, we discover how to find healing for our broken, angry souls. We can also offer a little of God's healing grace to the people who were so hurt that they hurt us.

Why would you settle for being a victim, knowing whom to blame, when you can be healed, knowing whom to praise?

The only way to make it to grateful living is to realize that it's just not about you. That isn't meant to demean you, but to free you. It frees you from allowing life's disappointments and hurts to determine your identity.

Best of all, it frees you to receive the creativity of God's grace that can be found even in the hurt. It isn't about you.

It is always about God.

—M. CRAIG BARNES IN *SACRED THIRST* (ZONDERVAN)

Suffering with a Purpose

It is when we view our suffering as meaningless—without purpose—that we are tempted to despair. A woman who endures the travail of childbirth is able to do it because she knows that the end result will be a new life.

Those who are terminally ill do not have the same hope of a good result as in childbearing. Here the pain appears to be unto death rather than unto life. Indeed that would be true if there is no salvation. If death is the end then the suffering that attends it would drive us to full and final despair. The message of Christ is that death is not unto death but unto life. The analogy of childbirth applies. It is used to describe the suffering of Christ and of the whole creation: "He shall see the travail of his soul and be satisfied" (Isa. 53:11).

—R. C. SPROUL IN *SURPRISED BY SUFFERING* (TYNDALE)

The Power and the Certainty
Lesson 6

2 Corinthians 12:7-10

⁷To keep me from becoming conceited because of these surpassingly great revelations, there was given me a thorn in my flesh, a messenger of Satan, to torment me. ⁸Three times I pleaded with the Lord to take it away from me. ⁹But he said to me, "My grace is sufficient for you, for my power is made perfect in weakness." Therefore I will boast all the more gladly about my weaknesses, so that Christ's power may rest on me. ¹⁰That is why, for Christ's sake, I delight in weaknesses, in insults, in hardships, in persecutions, in difficulties. For when I am weak, then I am strong.

Romans 8:12-21

¹²Therefore, brothers, we have an obligation—but it is not to the sinful nature, to live according to it. ¹³For if you live according to the sinful nature, you will die; but if by the Spirit you put to death the misdeeds of the body, you will live, ¹⁴because those who are led by the Spirit of God are sons of God. ¹⁵For you did not receive a spirit that makes you a slave again to fear, but you received the Spirit of sonship. And by him we cry, "Abba, Father." ¹⁶The Spirit himself testifies with our spirit that we are God's children. ¹⁷Now if we are children, then we are heirs—heirs of God and co-heirs with Christ, if indeed we share in his sufferings in order that we may also share in his glory.

¹⁸I consider that our present sufferings are not worth comparing with the glory that will be revealed in us. ¹⁹The creation waits in eager expectation for the sons of God to be revealed. ²⁰For the creation was subjected to frustration, not by its own choice, but by the will of the one who subjected it, in hope ²¹that the creation itself will be liberated from its bondage to decay and brought into the glorious freedom of the children of God.

Romans 8:28-39

²⁸And we know that in all things God works for the good of those who love him, who have been called according to his purpose. ²⁹For those God foreknew he also predestined to be conformed to the likeness of his Son, that he might be the firstborn among many brothers. ³⁰And those he predestined, he also called; those he called, he also justified; those he justified, he also glorified.

³¹What, then, shall we say in response to this? If God is for us, who can be against us? ³²He who did not spare his own Son, but gave him up for us all—how will he not also, along with him, graciously give us all things? ³³Who will bring any charge against those whom God has chosen? It is God who justifies. ³⁴Who is he that condemns? Christ Jesus, who died—more than that, who was raised to life—is at the right hand of God and is also interceding for us. ³⁵Who shall separate us from the love of Christ? Shall trouble or hardship or persecution or famine or nakedness or danger or sword? ³⁶As it is written:

"For your sake we face death all
    day long;
  we are considered as sheep to
    be slaughtered."

³⁷No, in all these things we are more than conquerors through him who loved us. ³⁸For I am convinced that neither death nor life, neither angels nor demons, neither the present nor the future, nor any powers, ³⁹neither height nor depth, nor anything else in all creation, will be able to separate us from the love of God that is in Christ Jesus our Lord.

Questions

1. **Why do some of the world's most powerful people seem to be brought down by their own weakness?**

2. **2 Corinthians 12:7-10**
   a. What was the reason for this particular suffering, the "thorn in the flesh"?
   b. Where did this suffering come from?
   c. How did the Lord answer Paul's prayers?
   d. How could power be "made perfect in weakness"?
   e. What paradoxes do you see in this passage?

3. **Romans 8:12-21**
   a. Why do you think that people who seem to focus only on their selfish pleasures are characterized as "really living"?
   b. Whom does this passage say will really live?
   c. What blessings are connected with God's Spirit?
   d. How are suffering and glory connected in verses 17-18?
   e. How are other created things in a situation similar to ours?

4. **Romans 8:28-39**
   a. How many things has God done for his people, according to verses 28-30?
   b. Because our glorification is not complete, how do God's other actions on our behalf give us assurance?
   c. Complete this sentence: Since God gave up his Son for us, I know _____.
   d. Is there any human being or difficult situation that can separate a believer from Christ's love?

5. **Summary**
   a. What have you learned about power from this study?
   b. What are some absolute certainties for Christians who are suffering?

What to Pray For

For the salvation of our soul may we boldly pray. For grace may we boldly pray, for faith, for hope and for charity, and for every such virtue as shall serve us to heavenward. But as for all other things before remembered, in which is contained the matter of every kind of tribulation, we may never well make prayers so precisely but that we must express or imply a condition therein. That is to wit, that if God sees the contrary better for us, we refer it whole to His will, and instead of our grief taking away, pray that God may send us of his goodness either spiritual comfort to take it gladly, or strength at the least wise to bear it patiently.

—ST. THOMAS MORE IN *A DIALOGUE OF COMFORT AGAINST TRIBULATION*

Fred and the Rock

Within a six-month period of time, Fred Whiteman lost his best friend, who died with cancer of the liver, his mother died, and his wife died, having gone to work perfectly healthy one morning and then dying later that day in what most would term a "freakish accident." In addition to that, Fred's heart failed him; and even then, following a successful heart transplant, Fred himself faced surgery for cancer, as well as being sued by the bank where his wife worked.

The words of a popular song go, "When all hope is gone, go into your room and turn on a sad song." Instead, Fred did what the psalmist recommended, who cried out, "When my heart is overwhelmed, lead me to the rock that is higher than I" (Ps. 61:2). "I never had a moment," says Fred, "when there was no hope!"

Why should one have so many difficulties? Fred doesn't fully understand, but neither is he spending time trying to solve that question. He quickly says that difficulty does several things for a per-son: (1) It gives you a knowledge of yourself that also makes you aware of your intense need for God. It makes you fully understand your humanity and the fact that we live one heartbeat away from eternity. (2) Difficulty produces character in your life and refines the integrity of the heart. It strips you of the desire to play games and pretend to be what you are not. (3) And it allows God to use you as a witness to other people, showing them that at the point of our deep need, God can and does meet His children.

When Fred was asked to talk with three different psychiatrists, one of whom had asked why he just didn't commit suicide, Fred began to explain his relationship with Jesus Christ. All three psychiatrists, professionals who deal with grief and difficulty every day, were left in tears.

Fred doesn't understand why some face difficulty and grow with it, as he has, and why some face similar circumstances and wither. But he does know that God will meet you at the point of your deepest need. He's been there and learned that firsthand.

—HAROLD J. SALA IN *HEROES: PEOPLE WHO MADE A DIFFERENCE IN OUR WORLD* (PROMISE PRESS)

The Power to Overcome

I remember a time in my life when I was going through pain and suffering unlike any I had ever known. At one point I happened to read some words I had seen many times before:

O love that will not let me go,
   I rest my weary soul in thee:
I give thee back the life I owe,
   That in thine ocean depths its
      flow
May richer, fuller, be.

In the midst of the greatest heartache I had ever known, I saw a depth of meaning in those words which, though I had seen them a thousand times before, I had never grasped.

Christ gives us the power to overcome. He has delivered; he does deliver; he will yet deliver us.

Beyond Good Friday lies Easter morning. Beyond the agony of the crucifixion lies the glory of the resurrection. Beyond the sorrow of this vale of tears lies the splendor of paradise. Whatever comes to us, God will enable us to endure it. What a magnificent certainty! How sweet indeed are the uses of adversity!

—D. JAMES KENNEDY IN *TURN IT TO GOLD* (SERVANT)

Not by Your Power

Obedience to the call of Jesus never lies within our own power. If, for instance, we give away all our possessions, that act is not in itself the obedience he demands. In fact such a step might be the precise opposite of obedience to Jesus, for we might then be choosing a way of life for ourselves, some Christian ideal, or some ideal of Franciscan poverty. Indeed in the very act of giving away his goods a man can give allegiance to himself and to an ideal and not to the command of Jesus. He is not set free from his own self but still more enslaved to himself. The step into the situation where faith is possible is not an offer which we can make to Jesus but always his gracious offer to us. Only when the step is taken in the Spirit is it admissible. But in that case we cannot speak of a freedom of choice on our part.

—DIETRICH BONHOEFFER IN *THE COST OF DISCIPLESHIP* (MACMILLAN)

Eyes on the Prize

Lesson 7

Hebrews 11:6-19

⁶And without faith it is impossible to please God, because anyone who comes to him must believe that he exists and that he rewards those who earnestly seek him.

⁷By faith Noah, when warned about things not yet seen, in holy fear built an ark to save his family. By his faith he condemned the world and became heir of the righteousness that comes by faith.

⁸By faith Abraham, when called to go to a place he would later receive as his inheritance, obeyed and went, even though he did not know where he was going. ⁹By faith he made his home in the promised land like a stranger in a foreign country; he lived in tents, as did Isaac and Jacob, who were heirs with him of the same promise. ¹⁰For he was looking forward to the city with foundations, whose architect and builder is God.

¹¹By faith Abraham, even though he was past age—and Sarah herself was barren—was enabled to become a father because he considered him faithful who had made the promise. ¹²And so from this one man, and he as good as dead, came descendants as numerous as the stars in the sky and as countless as the sand on the seashore.

¹³All these people were still living by faith when they died. They did not receive the things promised; they only saw them and welcomed them from a distance. And they admitted that they were aliens and strangers on earth. ¹⁴People who say such things show that they are looking for a country of their own. ¹⁵If they had been thinking of the country they had left, they would have had opportunity to return. ¹⁶Instead, they were longing for a better country—a heavenly one. Therefore God is not ashamed to be called their God, for he has prepared a city for them.

¹⁷By faith Abraham, when God tested him, offered Isaac as a sacrifice. He who had received the promises was about to sacrifice his one and only son, ¹⁸even though God had said to him, "It is through Isaac that your offspring will be reckoned." ¹⁹Abraham reasoned that God could raise the dead, and figuratively speaking, he did receive Isaac back from death.

Hebrews 11:24-27, 35b-40

²⁴By faith Moses, when he had grown up, refused to be known as the son of Pharaoh's daughter. ²⁵He chose to be mistreated along with the people of God rather than to enjoy the pleasures of sin for a short time. ²⁶He regarded disgrace for the sake of Christ as of greater value than the treasures of Egypt, because he was looking ahead to his reward. ²⁷By faith he left Egypt, not fearing the king's anger; he persevered because he saw him who is invisible.

³⁵ᵇOthers were tortured and refused to be released, so that they might gain a better resurrection. ³⁶Some faced jeers and flogging, while still others were chained and put in prison. ³⁷They were stoned; they were sawed in two; they were put to death by the sword. They went about in sheepskins and goatskins, destitute, persecuted and mistreated—³⁸the world was not worthy of them. They wandered in deserts and mountains, and in caves and holes in the ground.

³⁹These were all commended for their faith, yet none of them received what had been promised. ⁴⁰God had planned something better for us so that only together with us would they be made perfect.

Hebrews 12:1-3

¹Therefore, since we are surrounded by such a great cloud of witnesses, let us throw off everything that hinders and the sin that so easily entangles, and let us run with perseverance the race marked out for us. ²Let us fix our eyes on Jesus, the author and perfecter of our faith, who for the joy set before him endured the cross, scorning its shame, and sat down at the right hand of the throne of God. ³Con- sider him who endured such opposition from sinful men, so that you will not grow weary and lose heart.

Questions

1. **Who was your favorite teacher? Why?**

2. **Hebrews 11:6-19**
   a. What must we believe about God?
   b. How hard would it have been for Noah to make a radical change in his life to prepare for a flood never before imagined?
   c. What motivated Abraham to move his family to a distant land?
   d. Why did Abraham and Sarah believe the impossible?
   e. For these people of faith, how did their knowledge that they would live forever affect how they viewed their time on earth?
   f. How was Abraham's faith severely tested?

3. **Hebrews 11:24-27, 35b-40**
   a. What did Moses give up?
   b. Based on verses 35-40, would you say that Christianity is a religion looking to attract people with "easy believism"?

4. **Hebrews 12:1-3**
   a. In addition to being good examples and mentors to us, what else are those heroes of the faith?
   b. Describe how the Christian life is like a race.
   c. Who is already at the finish line, coaching us?

5. **Summary**
   a. After today's study, how would you define faith?
   b. What did the people of faith we read about seem to have in common with one another?
   c. What did the heroes of faith understand that many people today don't seem to understand, based on how they live?

Foolish to Follow Him?

[John Wooden's] UCLA teams won ten NCAA championships in 12 years. . . . No one speaks more eloquently about Wooden than Bill Walton, who played for UCLA at a troubled time in America, a time of Vietnam and Watergate, a time when young people were asking hard questions, when dissent was in style.

For Wooden, the answers never changed. "We thought he was nuts," Walton said. "But in all his preachings and teachings, everything he told us turned out to be true. . . ."

"His interest and goal was to make you the best basketball player but first to make you the best person," Walton said. "He would never talk wins and losses but what we needed to succeed in life. Once you were a good human being, you had a chance to be a good player. He never deviated from that.

"He never tried to be your friend. He was your teacher, your coach. He handled us with extreme patience. . . ."

Today, Walton talks with the 90-year-old Wooden frequently. "He has thousands of maxims. He is more John Wooden today than ever. He is a man who truly has principles and ideas. . . .

"He didn't teach basketball. He taught life."

—HAL BOCK WRITING IN *THE SPOKANE-REVIEW* (DEC. 4, 2000)

Hunger for God

The cost of food in the kingdom is hunger for the bread of heaven, instead of the white bread of the world. Do you want it? Are you hungry? Or are you satisfied with yourself and your television and your computer and your job and your family?

—JOHN PIPER, FROM THE SERMON "THE PRESENT POWER OF A FUTURE POSSESSION"

Following the Leader

A smoker for 25 years, my friend's father, an Army sergeant, tried repeatedly to quit. At his annual medical exam, the Army doctor told him that his health was being severely harmed by smoking and that he should stop. The sergeant confessed he knew he should stop and, in a tone of despair, related his many attempts over many years.

The physician looked at him and said, "What are these two bars on my lapel?"

"They mean you are a captain," the sergeant replied.

"Yes," said the captain, "And they also mean I outrank you, and I am giving you a direct order to stop smoking."

My friend's father never smoked another cigarette. He could not quit on his own, even after years of trying, but he could quit when he understood the power of a direct order from a superior officer.

As believers in Christ, we have received many commands from our Commander-in-Chief. When we take them seriously, we'll be surprised how God can transform our lives.

—LEADERSHIP

A Father's Care

As Hudson Taylor began the impossible task of evangelizing inland China, he was told: "You will be forgotten. . . . With no committee or organization before the public, you will be lost sight of in that distant land. Claims are many nowadays. Before long you may find yourselves without even the necessaries of life!"

"I am taking my children with me," was the quiet answer, "and I notice it is not difficult to remember that they need breakfast in the morning, dinner at midday, and supper at night. Indeed, I could not forget them if I tried. And I find it impossible to think that our heavenly Father is less tender and mindful of his children than I, a poor earthly father, am of mine. No, he will not forget us!"

—ELIZABETH SKOGLUND IN *WOUNDED HEROES* (BAKER)

Mentors: Be One or Find One

Even though Rodger and Lynne Schmidt were planning to go to Africa as missionaries, they found themselves asking, "Is this really something we should be doing?"

At the same time in the same city, another couple was also wrestling with their call, though from the other end of a missionary career. Now retired, this couple was asking, "After 41 years as missionaries in Africa, who are we? Our home and life work are on another continent. What is our life all about?"

God (through a mentoring program at Denver Seminary) brought these two couples together. It was a great match. The Schmidts' call was confirmed, and the retired couple discovered significance in their new role as mentors.

"We felt encouraged, they felt validated," Schmidt says. Both couples experienced the benefits of mentoring.

Why do the trades have apprenticeships and medical professions require internships? Because personal attention from experienced practitioners helps learners master essential skills, attitudes, and knowledge. This, of course, is no surprise to Christians familiar with the mentoring relationships of Moses and Joshua, Elijah and Elisha, Naomi and Ruth, Paul and Timothy, and Jesus and the disciples.

A mentor is "a brain to pick, an ear to listen, and a push in the right direction," according to The Uncommon Individual Foundation, an organization devoted to mentoring research and training. It reports that mentoring is the third most powerful relationship for influencing human behavior, after marriage and the extended family.

—ERIK JOHNSON IN *LEADERSHIP*